Contents

The game 2
The laws 2
The ground 3
The ball 4
Players 4
Duration of play 6

Start of play 7
Choice of end 7
Kick-off 8

Open play 9
Handling 9
Tackling 10

Kicking 12
Punt 12
Grubber kick 12
Drop kick 12
Place kick 13
Free kick 14
Penalty kick 15

Dead ball 17
Touch 17
Touch-in-goal 17

Line-out/throw in 18
Throw in 18
Line-out 19

Scrum 20

Ruck and maul 23

Scoring 26
Try 26
Goal 27

Officials 29
Referee 29
Touch judge 30

Offences 31
Offside in open play 31
Ball touching referee 36
Obstruction 37
Misconduct and dangerous play 37

Variations of the game 38
Seven-a-side 38
Mini and midi rugby 38
New image rugby 44
Under-13 to under-19 rugby 45

The Rugby Football Union 47

Index 48

The game

Acknowledgements

Thanks to Keith Bonser and Jim Crowe. The publishers would like to thank James Gilbert Ltd for its photographic contribution to this book.

All action photography courtesy of Colorsport.
Illustrations by Ron Dixon.

Note Throughout the book players and officials are referred to individually as 'he'. This should, of course, be taken to mean 'he or she' where appropriate.

The game of rugby union is played by two teams, each with 15 players. It is normally played on grass; it is possible to play on other surfaces, such as sand or soft clay, as long as these do not make the playing of the game dangerous. The object of the game is to score tries and kick goals (*see* pages 26-8). A try is scored by a player grounding the ball in his opponents' in-goal, and a goal is scored by kicking the ball between the opponents' goal posts above the cross-bar.

The laws

The laws of rugby union are framed and interpreted by the International Rugby Football Board (IRFB). They are binding on all matches, except some domestic ones, played in the countries represented on the Board.

The ground

Fig. 1 shows the markings and dimensions of the playing area. The size of the playing area should be as near as practicable to the maximum dimensions indicated in fig. 1; it includes the field of play, which is bounded by but does not include the goal lines and touch lines, and the in-goal.

Marking lines should be clearly defined and uniform in width, made with whiting or chalk and not more than 10 cm wide. Ruts should not be cut in the turf.

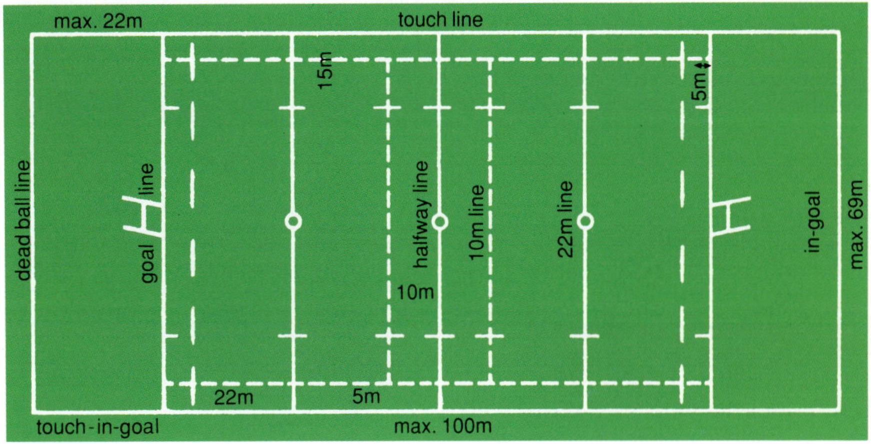

▲ *Fig. 1 Markings and dimensions of the playing area*

The goal

The goal is made of two upright posts, 5.6 m apart, joined by a cross-bar 3 m off the ground, and stands in the centre of the goal line. For the purposes of judging a kick at goal, the upright posts are considered to extend indefinitely upwards, and thus the taller the posts the easier the task of the adjudicating official.

Flag posts

Flag posts are placed at the corners of the goal lines and touch lines, and to mark the 22 m and halfway lines. They also mark the corners of the dead ball lines and the touch-in-goal lines. In the case of those marking the halfway and 22 m lines, the flag posts are normally placed approximately 1 m outside the touch line.

The posts should be upright (and a minimum of 1.2 m high) but not too firmly fixed, so that they will give way if a player falls against them.

The ball

The game is played with an oval four-panelled ball, the outer casing enclosing an air-inflated bladder. It must have the following dimensions:

- weight: 400-440 g
- length in line: 280-300 mm
- circumference (end on): 760-790 mm
- circumference (in width): 580-620 mm.

Nothing should be used in the construction which might injure the players. The lacing, if there is any, should be given careful consideration so that the outer casing is neatly closed.

▲ *Ball*

Players

The names of the positions occupied by the players, and the numbers worn by them, are governed by IRFB regulations. They are shown in fig. 2 on page 5, along with the line-up for a scrum. No. 9, the scrum half, is the player who usually puts the ball in the scrum. No. 2, the hooker, is the player who attempts to 'rake' the ball from the scrum with his foot.

The team consists of:

forward unit	front row forwards (nos 1, 2 & 3) second row forwards (nos 4 & 5) back row forwards (nos 6, 7 & 8)
back unit	half backs (nos 9 & 10) three-quarter backs (nos 11, 12, 13 & 14) full back (no. 15)

Replacements and substitutes

A player who has a bleeding or open wound must be replaced temporarily until the bleeding is controlled and the wound dressed. Other injured players may be replaced permanently and must NOT resume playing. Up to two substitutes of front row players and up to four substitutes of other players may be made for any other reason. A previously substituted player may resume playing only if he is needed to replace a player with a bleeding wound, or an injured front row player for whom no other suitably trained replacement is available.

In international matches up to six players may be nominated as replacements/substitutes (seven players in under-21 teams). In other matches the number is decided by the Union under whose authority the match is played.

If a front row forward is ordered off and there is no other player on the field able to play in the front row, the captain may nominate one other forward to leave the field and be replaced by a substitute front row forward.

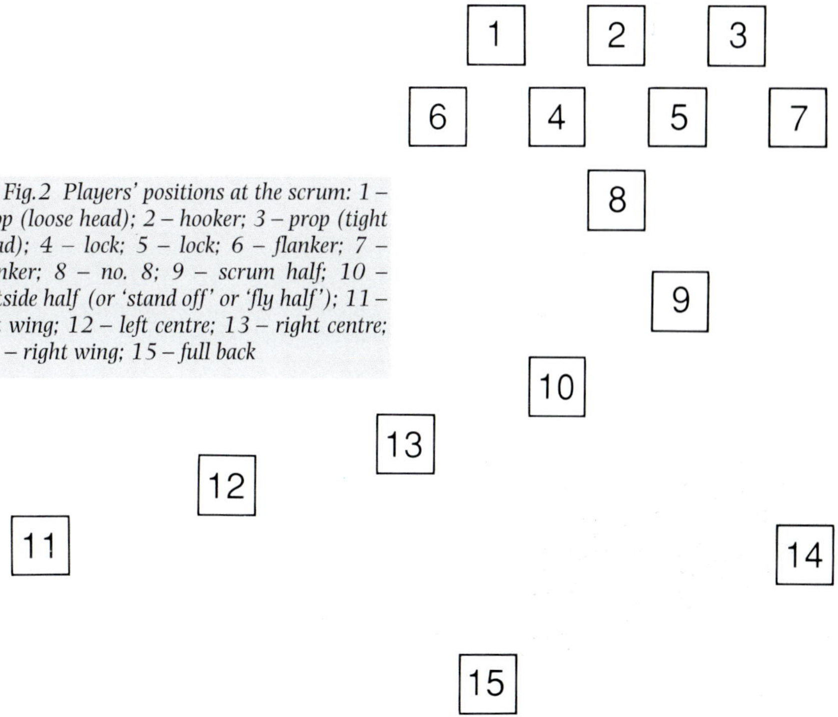

Fig.2 Players' positions at the scrum: 1 – prop (loose head); 2 – hooker; 3 – prop (tight head); 4 – lock; 5 – lock; 6 – flanker; 7 – flanker; 8 – no. 8; 9 – scrum half; 10 – outside half (or 'stand off' or 'fly half'); 11 – left wing; 12 – left centre; 13 – right centre; 14 – right wing; 15 – full back

Clothing

The players of each team wear shirts and shorts of the same colour. The shirts are usually numbered, each number indicating the position of the wearer (*see* fig. 2 on page 5).

Players should be smart in appearance. A smart team is not necessarily a good team, but a good team is invariably of smart appearance.

▲ *Boots*

Footwear

A player should take great care of his boots, cleaning them thoroughly and keeping the leather in good condition. Studs must be securely fastened. Long studs are more useful than short ones on soft grounds, but they must not be more than 1.8 cm in length. The wearing of a single stud at the toe of the boot is prohibited.

The referee can order a player to remove any part of his equipment which is likely to cause injury to other players, e.g. projecting nails on boots, rings on fingers, buckles, leather shoulder pads.

Duration of play

In international matches the game lasts for two periods of 40 minutes each. In other matches the duration of the game is agreed upon by the respective teams, up to a maximum of two periods of 40 minutes each.

Play is divided into two halves, separated by an interval of not more than ten minutes. At half-time the teams change ends.

The referee blows his whistle to indicate half-time and the end of the game ('no-side'), but to do so he must wait for the ball to become 'dead'. If a try has been scored, or a penalty kick, free kick, scrum or line-out has been awarded, the referee must allow play to continue until the ball becomes dead again before blowing for half-time or the end of the game.

Start of play

Choice of end

Before the game starts the home captain tosses a coin, and the visiting captain calls. The winner of the toss may choose:

(a) to kick off, or
(b) which goal line his team will defend in the first half.

If he chooses (b), his opponents take the kick-off. After the half-time interval, the kick-off is taken by the opposite team to that which started the game.

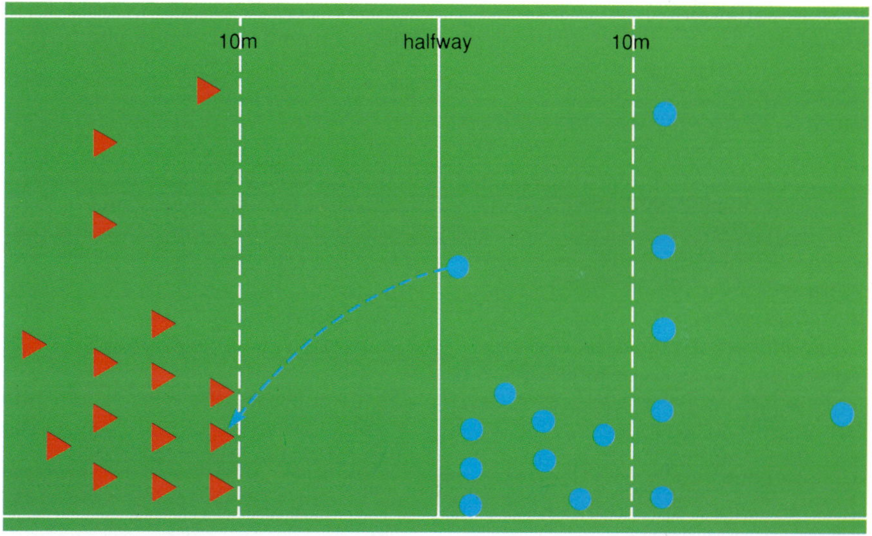

▲ *Fig. 3 The kick-off*

Kick-off

After the choice of end, the teams line up in their respective halves of the field, and the game begins with a place kick, taken by any player of the team awarded the kick-off. The ball is placed at the centre of the halfway line, and must be kicked forwards in the direction of the opponents' 10 m line. The ball can be placed on the ground, on a small pile of sand or sawdust, or on an approved kicking tee. All players of the kicker's team must remain behind the halfway line until the ball has been kicked forwards.

The ball must reach the opponents' 10 m line, unless an opponent plays it first. If not, and subject to advantage (*see* page 30), it is either kicked off again or a scrum is formed at the centre, at the opponents' discretion. The team receiving the kick-off must be behind and remain behind its 10 m line until the ball is kicked, otherwise the kick is taken again.

If the ball pitches directly into touch (without touching the ground), the team receiving the kick-off has three choices:

- it can accept the kick and take the line-out. This line-out will be taken either at the halfway line, or from where the ball went out of play, if that is nearer the kicker's goal line
- it can have the kick taken again
- it can take a scrum at the centre spot.

If the ball goes into in-goal, the receiving team has three choices:

- to play on
- to ground the ball, and take a scrum at the centre spot
- to have the kick taken again.

If the ball goes over the dead ball line or into touch-in-goal, the receiving team takes a scrum at the centre.

After half-time, the game is restarted in the same way.

After a score, the game restarts with a drop kick taken at the centre spot. All the other conditions listed above apply to this kick.

Open play

Handling

The ball may be passed, thrown or knocked from one player to another in any direction except a forward one.

Forward pass

If a player unintentionally throws the ball in a forward direction to one of his own team, the referee awards a scrum at the place where the infringement occurred.

If the throw is not forward, but the ball falls to the ground and then bounces forwards, it is not an infringement and play continues.

Knock-on

A knock-on occurs when:

- a player loses possession of the ball, and the ball goes forwards (towards the opponents' dead ball line)
- a player fails to catch the ball before it touches the ground (or another player), and the ball goes forwards off his hand or arm
- the ball hits a player on the hand or arm and goes forwards to touch the ground or another player before he can catch it.

A knock-on does not occur when the ball travels forwards from the hands or arms of a player who is charging down a kick, as long as he is not trying to catch the ball.

When a knock-on is not intentional, the non-offending team takes a scrum from where the infringement occurred. If, however, the knock-on is intentional, the offender is penalised with a penalty kick.

Rebound

If the ball strikes any part of a player's body other than his hand or arm, and then travels in the direction of his opponents' dead ball line, it is said to have 'rebounded'. Play continues, without interruption.

Should the ball touch a player's hand or arm and then strike another part of his body before travelling forwards, it is a rebound and not a knock-on.

If the ball strikes a player's leg (from the knee to the toe inclusive), the player is deemed to have kicked the ball.

Tackling

A player is tackled:

- when he is carrying the ball and is held by his opponent(s), and 'brought to the ground'
- when he is held and the ball touches the ground.

The ball carrier is 'brought to the ground' if he is held and:
– has one or both knees on the ground
– is sitting on the ground
– is on top of another player who is on the ground.

A player is not tackled if:

- he is lifted off both feet by an opponent
- he is knocked or thrown over without being held even if the ball touches the ground.

The player may therefore pass or release the ball or get up and continue his run.

If the momentum of a player who has been tackled carries him with the ball into his opponents' in-goal, and he grounds the ball there, the referee should award a try.

A tackled player must pass or release the ball at once. When he is 'brought to the ground' he and the tackler must attempt to get away from the ball immediately. Any player on the ground after a tackle must get to his feet before he can take any further part in play.

After the tackled player has released the ball, all other players must be on their feet when they play the ball.

Handing off

A player may avoid or break a tackle by 'handing off' his opponent. The hand-off must be made with a push of the open palm of the hand; a player must not strike an opponent with a clenched fist.

Falling on the ball

No player may wilfully fall on or over a player lying on the ground with the ball in his possession or close to him.

It is illegal for a player to fall on or over the ball as it comes out of a scrum or ruck.

Kicking

Punt

A player punts the ball when he drops it from his hand(s) and kicks it into the air before it touches the ground. Useful for finding touch or gaining ground, but a goal cannot be scored from it.

The ball is kicked with the extended foot, off the laces of the boot, and an expert can impart a spin to the ball which gives the kick extra length and accuracy (known as a 'screw kick'). This spin is imparted by placing the ball at an angle across the line of the kicking foot.

Grubber kick

A player grub kicks the ball when he drops it from his hand(s) and kicks it so that it is driven forwards bouncing over the ground. The grubber kick is useful to drive the ball between opponents who are in close proximity to the kicker, or to find touch when the kicker is outside his 22 m area.

Drop kick

A player drop kicks the ball when he lets it fall from his hand(s) to the ground, and kicks it immediately it rebounds. A drop kick is used to:

- restart the game at the centre after a score
- restart the game at the 22 m line after a touch down, or after the ball has gone into touch-in-goal or over the dead ball line
- kick at goal after a try has been scored
- score a goal during play.

Place kick

For a place kick the ball is kicked from on the ground, or from a small pile of sand or sawdust, or from an approved kicking tee. It is used to:

- start the game, and to recommence it after the interval
- kick at goal after a try has been scored, in which case the kick is taken from any spot opposite where the try was scored and parallel to the touch line.

There are various ways of place kicking favoured by players; the two most popular are shown in figs 4 and 5. A good kicker takes infinite care at a place kick, and after sighting the goal does not take his eye off the ball until he has kicked it.

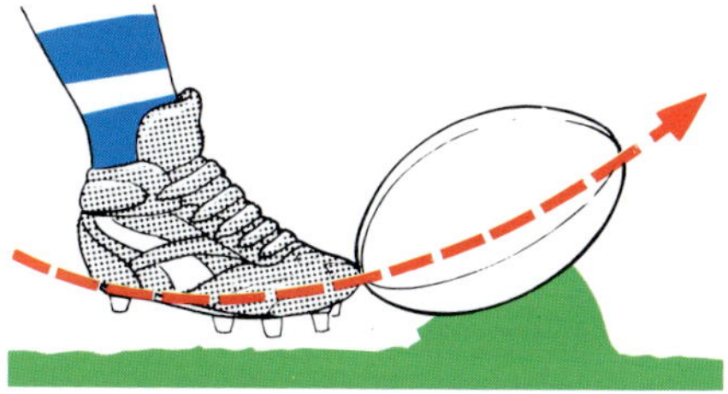

▲ *Fig.4 Kicking with the toe of the boot*

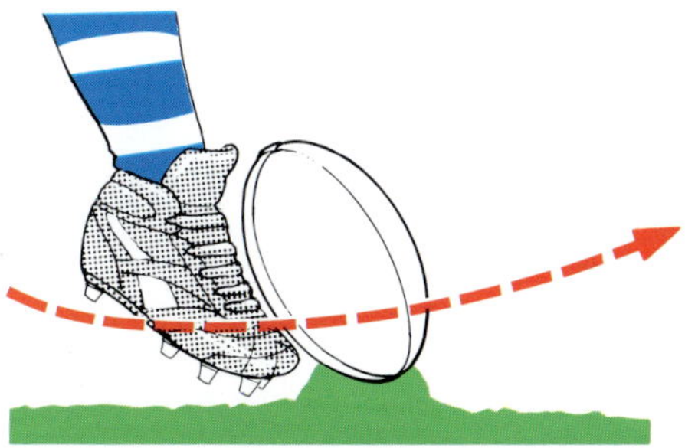

▲ *Fig.5 Kicking with the instep*

Free kick

A free kick is awarded:

- for a 'fair catch'
- for particular infringements of the law.

A fair catch is made by a player who, while in his own in-goal or 22 m area, catches the ball cleanly from an opponent's kick and calls 'Mark!' as he makes the catch.

A free kick for a fair catch must be taken by the player who made the mark: if he cannot do so within a minute of making the mark, his team must take a scrum.

A free kick awarded for an infringement of the law can be taken by any player.

The free kick must be taken at or behind the place where the mark was made or where the infringement occurred, on a line parallel to the touch line. Any kick must be taken at least 5 m from the goal line.

A team cannot score a goal from a free kick, and cannot score a drop goal until the ball has next become dead or an opponent has played it or has tackled an opponent or a maul has formed.

The kicker can kick the ball in any direction. If he is kicking for touch, he can only use the punt or the drop kick. If he is taking a quick free kick he must visibly kick the ball.

With the exception of the quick free kick, the players in the kicker's team must be behind the ball until it is kicked.

At the free kick, the players in the opposing team must run backwards towards the goal line until they are 10 m away from the mark.

As soon as the kicker starts his run or offers to kick, the opposing team, from 10 m away, can run to charge down the kick or prevent it being taken. If the kick is charged down, play continues. If the opponents prevent the kick - by tackling the kicker, for example - the referee will award them a scrum at the mark.

If there is an infringement of the law by the kicker's team, the referee awards a scrum to the opposition.

If there is an infringement by the opposing team, the referee will award a second free kick 10 m ahead of the first mark.

Quick free kick ('tap free kick')

A player can take a quick free kick without waiting for his team mates to get behind the ball, but these players must continue to retire until they are onside. They will be put onside either when they get behind the ball or when the player carrying the ball has run past them.

When the quick free kick is taken, the opposing players within 10 m of the ball must retire and continue to do so until they are 10 m away, or until one of their own team who was at least 10 m away has run in front of them.

A team may choose to take a scrum instead of a free kick.

Penalty kick

A penalty kick may be a drop kick, a place kick, a tap or a punt. It is taken at the mark or at any point directly behind the mark where the infringement occurred, but not within 5 m of the opponents' goal line.

The object of the kick may be:

- to score a goal from a drop kick or place kick
- to gain ground by kicking for touch, in which case a place kick may not be used
- to gain ground and attempt to gain possession by kicking forwards for the kicker's team to follow up if onside.

The kicker can kick the ball in any direction, and play it again without restriction.

When the penalty kick is taken, the following rules must be observed:

- all players of the kicker's team, other than the placer for a place kick, must be behind the ball when it is kicked. However, a quick kick may be taken without waiting for players of the kicker's team to retire behind the ball provided that those players continue to retire and do not enter the game until they are onside. Otherwise, if a player is in front of the ball when it is kicked, a scrum is formed at the original position
- players of the defending team must retire without delay to a position 10 m from where the kick is being taken, or to their own goal line, whichever is nearer
- if a kick at goal is being taken, players of the defending team must stand motionless, with their hands by their sides, until the ball has been kicked.

For an infringement by the opposing team, the kicker's team is given another kick 10 m in front of the mark or 5 m from the goal line, whichever is the nearer, on a line through the mark parallel to the touch line.

The following points relating to a penalty kick should be noted:

- the non-offending team may choose to take a scrum instead of a penalty kick
- no penalty kick can be taken closer than 5 m from the opponents' goal line.

Quick penalty kick ('tap penalty kick')

A player can take a quick penalty kick without waiting for his team mates to get behind the ball, but these players must continue to retire until they are onside. They will be put onside either when they get behind the ball or when the player carrying the ball has run past them.

When the quick penalty kick is taken, the opposing players within 10 m of the ball must retire and continue to do so until they are 10 m away, or until one of their own team who was at least 10 m away has run in front of them.

A team may choose to take a scrum instead of a penalty kick.

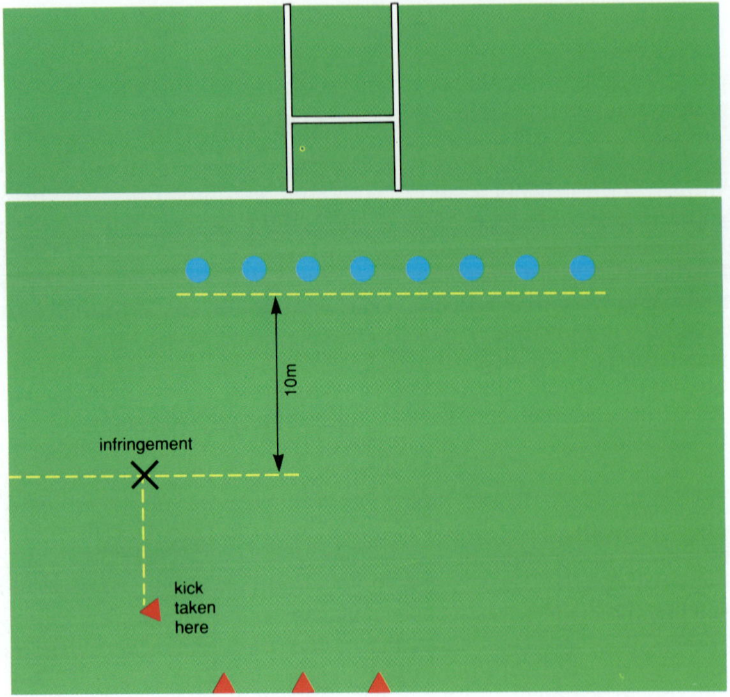

▲ *Fig.6 The penalty kick*

Dead ball

The ball is 'dead' when it is out of play. This occurs:

- when it has gone out of the playing area. It can go out of play:
– over the touch line, and the game is restarted with a line-out (*see* page 19), or
– into the in-goal area and touched down by a defender, or over the dead ball line. In this case, if the attacking team last touched the ball, the game is restarted with a drop kick at the 22 m line. If a player in the defending team last touched the ball, the game is restarted with a 5 m scrum to the attacking side. If a player deliberately throws the ball out of play, the referee will award a penalty kick to the opposing team
- when the referee blows his whistle for an infringement
- when a conversion kick after a try has been taken.

Touch

The ball is in touch when:

- it touches the ground on or over the touch line, or a person or object on or beyond it (the touch line itself being out of play)
- a player carrying it steps on or touches the touch line, or the ground outside it.

The ball is not in touch when:

- a player standing in touch kicks a ball which has not touched or crossed the touch line and is in the field of play
- it is blown out of the field of play and back in again without touching the ground.

Note A player is not allowed to throw the ball into touch deliberately, and should he do so a penalty kick is awarded against him.

Touch-in-goal

Touch-in-goal occurs when the ball or player carrying it touches a corner post, a touch-in-goal line, or the ground, a person or object on or beyond it. The flag itself is not regarded as part of the corner post.

Line-out/throw in

Throw in

When, in the normal course of play, the ball or a player carrying the ball goes into touch, a throw in is awarded to the opposing team. This may be taken as a quick throw in or as a formed line-out. However, if the ball is kicked directly into touch from a penalty kick, the kicking team throws in the ball.

When the ball is in touch, the place at which it must be thrown in is as follows:

- when the ball is in touch from a penalty kick or a kick within 22 m of the kicker's goal line – at the place where the ball went into touch
- if the ball pitches directly into touch after being kicked other than as stated above, or if the kicker has received the ball outside his 22 m line and retreated behind that line before kicking – opposite the place from which the ball was kicked, or at the place where it pitches into touch (if that place is nearer to the kicker's goal line)
- at a quick throw in – from any point between where the ball went into touch and the thrower's goal line
- on all other occasions when the ball is in touch (except for a quick throw in) – at the place where the ball went into touch.

Quick throw in

A quick throw in may be taken provided:

- the ball which went into touch is used
- the ball has been handled only by the thrower, and
- it is thrown in correctly.

Line-out

A line-out is formed by at least two players from each team, lining up in single parallel lines at right angles to the touch line.

The team throwing in the ball determines the maximum number of players from each team who are to line up – the opposition can have fewer, but not more. There must be a gap of 1 m between the two lines of players.

The line-out starts 5 m from the touch line where the ball is being thrown in, and can extend to a position up to 15 m from that touch line. Any player of either team who is further than 15 m away from the touch line when the line-out begins is not in the line-out. A player in the line-out can, however, move beyond the 15 m line to catch a long throw in, but he may move only after the ball has left the thrower's hands.

A player jumping for the ball must not be lifted but he may be supported above the waist by a member of his own team after he has jumped.

Pushing, charging or in any way interfering with an opponent in the line-out is prohibited unless that opponent has the ball in his possession, when he may lawfully be tackled.

The player taking the throw in must not step into the field of play. He must throw the ball in straight (down the line of touch), without feint, and it must travel at least 5 m before it touches the ground or is touched by a player.

If the throw in is taken incorrectly, the opposition can either take a second throw itself, or take a scrum 15 m from the touch line.

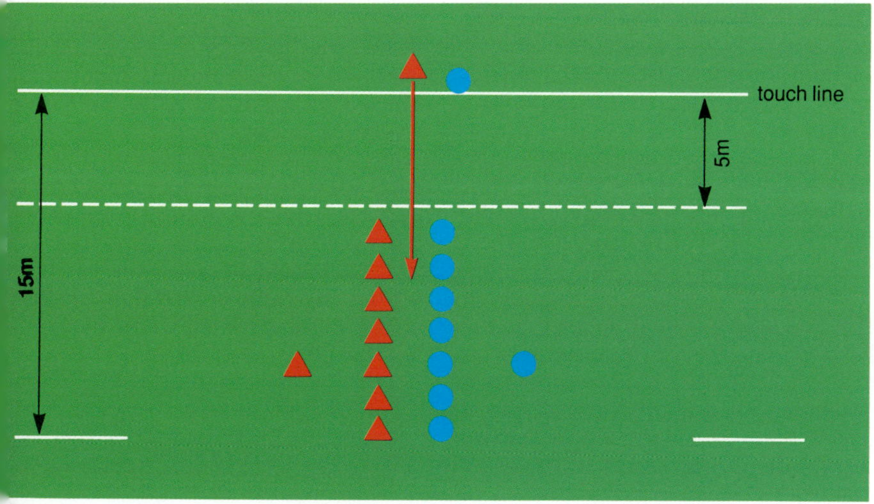

▲ *Fig. 7 Players' positions for the line-out*

Scrum

The scrum is ordered to restart the game after certain infringements. In most cases the scrum is formed where the infringement occurred. However, if this is within 5 m of the touch line, it is formed 5 m from that line. For infringements by a defending team in in-goal, the scrum is formed 5 m from the goal line. A scrum can only be formed in the field of play.

A scrum is formed by players of each team closing up for the ball to be put on the ground between them. A maximum of eight players from each team take part in the scrum; this number must not be exceeded while the scrum is taking place. All eight players must remain bound in the scrum until it ends.

There must be three players - no more, no less - bound together in the front row.

Before the front rows close together, at the mark indicated by the referee, the opposing players must be standing less than an arm's length apart. The ball must be in the scrum half's hands, ready to be put in.

The front row must crouch, so that when they close together each player's shoulders are no lower than his hips. They should come together when the referee calls 'Engage'. This call is not an order but an indication that the front rows may come together when ready.

The front rows must interlock so that no player's head is next to the head of a team mate. All other players in the scrum must bind with at least one arm and hand around the body of a team mate. The player whose feet are the 'hindmost' feet in the scrum must bind with at least one arm onto one of his locks.

Formations

There are two scrum formations which are adopted by teams: the 3–2–3 and 3–4–1 formations. The 3–4–1 formation is generally favoured, with variations such as 3–3–2 (*see* fig. 8) and 3–3–1, for forward link penetration with half backs. The advantages claimed for the 3–4–1 formation (*see* fig. 9) are:

- it is a stronger pushing unit, with the flankers fully contributing to the shove
- the ball can be heeled more quickly from the scrum
- when defending, the flankers are nearer to the opposition half backs.

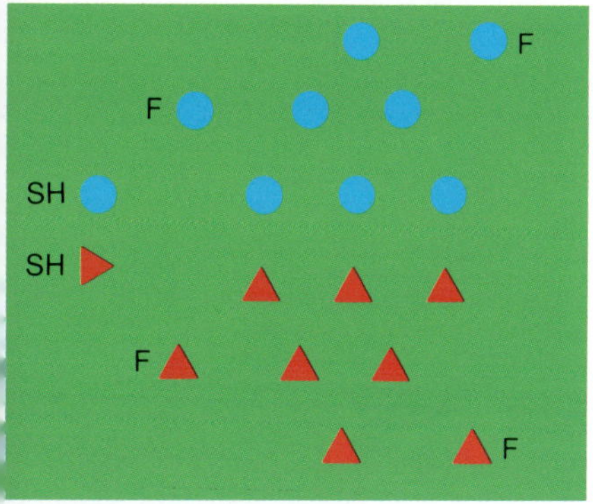

▲ *Fig.8 Scrum: 3–3–2 formation (SH = scrum half; F = flank forward)*

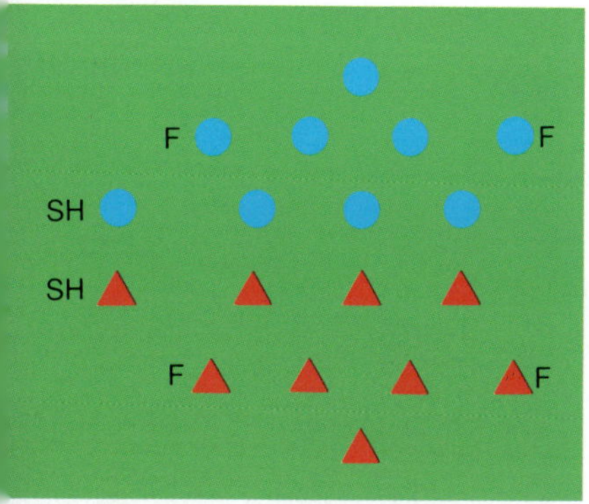

▲ *Fig.9 Scrum: 3–4–1 formation*

Putting in the ball

The player putting in the ball (usually the scrum half) must:

- stand 1 m from the scrum, on the middle line between the two front rows
- put in the ball with both hands, from a level midway between his knee and ankle, in a single forward movement
- pitch the ball on the ground immediately beyond the nearest player.

Until the ball has left the hands of the player putting it in, no player in either front row may raise either foot from the ground or advance it beyond the line of the feet of his front row. The feet of the nearest players must be far enough back to leave the tunnel clear.

When the ball has left the scrum half's hands and is fairly in the scrum, it may be played.

During the scrum

While the ball is in the scrum a player in the front row must not:

- raise both feet off the ground at the same time
- wilfully adopt any position or take any action, by twisting or lowering the body or by pulling on an opponent's clothing, which is likely to cause the scrum to collapse
- wilfully lift an opponent off his feet or force him upwards out of the scrum
- wilfully kick the ball out of the tunnel in the direction from which it is put in.

The referee must be strict in penalising the wilful collapsing of the scrum or the lifting of an opponent off his feet. If the ball comes out of the scrum at either end of the tunnel, he should order it to be put in again, or he may even award a free kick for wilfully kicking out.

Ruck and maul

A ruck, which can only take place on the field of play, is formed by one or more players from each team in physical contact and on their feet, closing round the ball when it is on the ground between them.

When the ball in a ruck becomes unplayable, a scrum is formed. In most cases the team moving forward before the stoppage will put the ball in.

Just as it is illegal to collapse a scrum or ruck, it is now illegal to collapse a maul.

A maul, which can also take place only on the field of play, is formed by one or more players from each team (at least three in total) on their feet and in physical contact, closing round a player who is carrying the ball. A maul ends when the ball is on the ground, the ball or a player carrying it emerges from the maul, or when a scrum is ordered.

When the ball becomes unplayable in a maul a scrum is formed. If the maul is formed around a player who has caught the ball from a kick other than a kick-off or drop-out, and who is immediately held by opponents so that the ball becomes unplayable, the catcher's team will put the ball into the scrum. In most other cases when the ball becomes unplayable in a maul, the team not in possession before the maul was formed will put the ball in.

There are two main differences between a ruck and a maul:

- the position of the ball: ruck – ball on ground; maul – ball carried
- whereas a ruck may have only two players, at least three are needed to form a maul.

In both rucks and mauls the head and shoulders of all players involved must be no lower than their hips.

Scrum and ruck infringements

In either a scrum or a ruck:

- a player must not return the ball into the scrum or ruck by hand or by foot after it has come out
- a player lying on the ground must not interfere with the ball in any way and must do his best to roll away from the ball
- a player must not handle the ball, pick it up by his hands and legs, or intentionally fall or kneel on it, unless the scrum or ruck has moved into either in-goal
- a player must not do anything to cause the scrum or ruck to collapse.

In a scrum:

- a player must not add himself to the front row to make more than three players in that row
- the player putting in the ball and his opposite number must not kick the ball while it is in the scrum, nor may they take any action while the ball is in the scrum to convey to the opponents that the ball is out.

Grounding the ball

A player grounds the ball in the in-goal area if he:

- brings the ball into contact with the ground while holding it in his hands or arms
- places his hand(s) or arm(s) on a ball which is on the ground in such a way that he exerts downward pressure on it
- falls on a ball which is on the ground so that it is anywhere under the front of his body, from waist to neck inclusive.

The purpose of grounding the ball for a defending player is to get out of a dangerous situation and cause a scrum or drop-out. The aim for an attacking player is to score a try.

Scoring

- A try scores five points.
- A goal converted from a try scores two points.
- A goal from a penalty kick or a drop kick scores three points.

The team with the higher number of points wins the match.

Try

A try is scored if an onside attacking player grounds the ball in his opponents' in-goal.

If, in a scrum or ruck, one team pushes the other over the defending team's goal line, the attacking team can score a try by grounding the ball.

The referee should award a penalty try to a player if, in his opinion, the player would probably have scored but for unfair play or unlawful interference by the defending team. In this case the try is awarded between the posts.

The goal line is itself within the in-goal area, so a player may score by grounding the ball on the goal line.

Goal

A goal may be scored by:

- converting a try (the conversion itself is worth two points, making seven in total)
- a penalty kick (three points)
- a drop kick during play (three points).

A goal is allowed if:

- the ball passes over the cross-bar and is then blown back by the wind
- the ball hits the cross-bar or goal posts and then rebounds over the cross-bar.

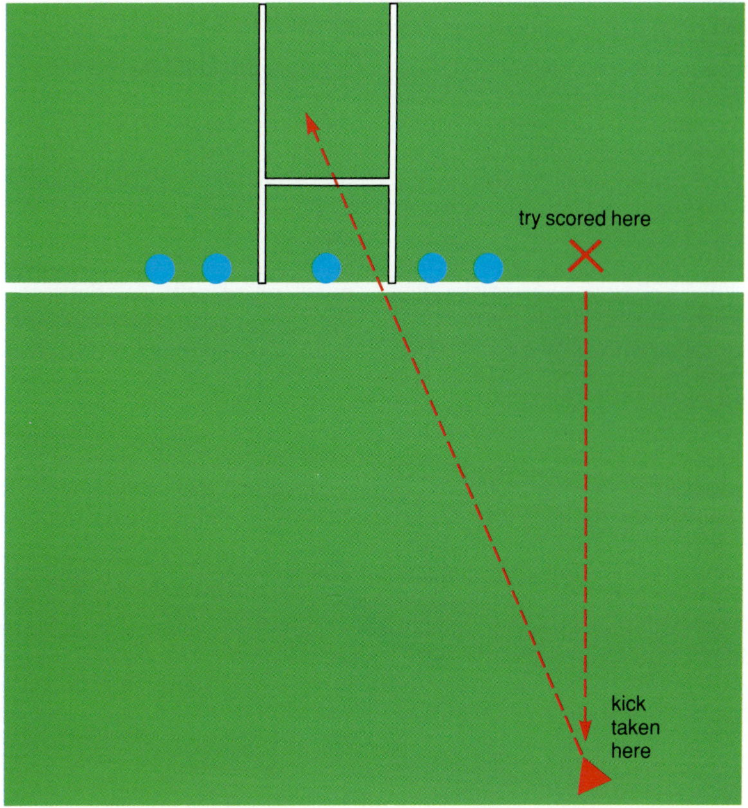

▲ *Fig. 10 Converting a try*

Converting a try

A team scoring a try is awarded a kick at goal, to attempt to 'convert' the try into a goal. A converted try scores seven points.

The kick at goal is taken at any point on an imaginary line parallel to the touch line and starting at the point where the try was awarded.

The kick may be a place kick or a drop kick. When a place kick is used, the kicker can place the ball on the ground, or on a small pile of sand or sawdust, or on an approved kicking tee. He can also have the ball held steady by another player if he thinks it necessary (i.e. in a high wind).

The attacking team normally retires to the halfway line for the restart of play while the kick is taken. The defending team must stand behind their own goal line until the kicker begins his run to kick. They may then charge or jump in an attempt to prevent the conversion.

The defending team restarts the game with a drop kick from the centre.

Goal from penalty kick

A team can attempt to kick a goal from a penalty awarded to it. If successful, this scores three points. The kick must be taken at the place where the offence occurred, or on a line directly behind it. It can be either a place kick or a drop kick.

All players of the offending team must retire without delay towards their own goal until they are 10 m from the spot where the offence occurred, or to their own goal line if that is nearer. They must stand still there, with their hands by their sides, until the ball has been kicked.

Players of the kicker's team remain behind the ball while the kick is taken.

Goal from drop kick

At any time during play, a player may drop kick the ball over the opponents' cross-bar. If successful (except following a free kick), this scores three points.

Officials

In all matches a referee and two touch judges must be appointed, or agreed upon by the two captains.

Referee

The referee is responsible for applying the laws of the game. He keeps the score and he is the timekeeper. In order to execute these duties he carries a whistle which he blows to stop play, a watch to keep time, and a card and pencil to keep score. He should also have a coin with which the two captains toss for choice of end. During the match the referee is the only judge of fact and law – all players must accept his decisions without question.

The referee's clothing should be of a colour easily distinguishable from that of the players.

The referee must order off any player who has already been cautioned for obstruction, foul play, misconduct or repeated infringement of the laws, and who then repeats the offence. Any player ordered off the field must be reported by the referee to the organisation under whose jurisdiction the game is being played.

If the referee is advised by a doctor or medically trained person, or for any other reasons considers a player to be so injured that it would be harmful for him to continue playing, the referee must ask the player to leave the field. A player who has left the field with an open or bleeding wound may now be temporarily replaced and can resume playing when the wound has been dressed.

When the referee has made a decision he cannot alter it, except:

- when he sees that a touch judge has his flag raised to show that the ball has gone out of play
- in certain important matches (e.g. international, representative and top class league and cup games), when qualified referees are appointed as touch judges, they can indicate to the referee that incidents of foul play or misconduct have occurred by pointing their flag towards the centre field.

In these two cases only can the referee alter his decision.

The success of the game can be enhanced by the referee, who should keep up with the play, be neutral yet consistent at all times in his decisions, and limit stoppages to a minimum.

Advantage law

The referee should not whistle for an infringement during play if a stoppage would deprive the non-offending team of any advantage and perhaps the opportunity to score; play should be allowed to continue.

The advantage law applies to every other law, with the following minor exceptions:

- if a team gains an advantage when the ball or a player carrying it touches the referee
- when the ball emerges from either end of the tunnel at a scrum without having been played.

Touch judge

The touch judge holds up his flag to show when and where the ball, or the player carrying it, went into touch or touch-in-goal. He indicates from which point and by which team the ball should be brought back into play. He lowers his flag when the ball has been thrown in properly.

The touch judge keeps his flag raised if:

- the ball is thrown in by a player of the team not entitled to do so
- the player throwing in the ball puts any part of either foot into the field of play
- at a quick throw in, the ball which went into touch is replaced by another or is handled by anyone other than the thrower.

In these cases, unless the opposing team has gained an advantage, that team has the option to throw in the ball or take a scrum.

The touch judge assists the referee to judge on kicks at goal by standing behind a goal post. If the ball goes over the crossbar he signals by raising his flag.

Fig.11 Touch judge's signals: goal (left); found touch (right); foul play (bottom)

Offences

Offside in open play

If a player is ruled to be offside, it means that he is temporarily out of the game. If he takes part in the game when offside he will be penalised. In general play, a player is in an offside position if he is in front of the team mate who has the ball, or in front of the team mate who last played the ball. In such a position he commits an offence if he:

- plays the ball or obstructs an opponent
- fails to retire without delay and without interference when he is within 10 m of an opponent waiting for the ball or of the place where the ball pitches
- moves towards the opponents waiting to play the ball or the place where the ball pitches, before he is put onside.

The referee will award a penalty kick to the opponents at the place where the offence occurred, or a scrum at the place where the ball was last played before it occurred. The non-offending team has the option of either award. There are two exceptions to this law.

- If one of the kicker's team moves in front of the kicker at the kick-off, at a drop-out, at a penalty kick or at a free kick (other than at a quick penalty or at a quick free kick), the referee will award a scrum to the opposition at the place where the kick was taken.
- When an offside player cannot avoid being touched by the ball, or a team mate carrying it, he is 'accidentally offside'. If his team gains no advantage, play continues; if his team does gain advantage, a scrum is awarded to the opposing team.

Offside at the scrum

At the scrum, the offside line for the scrum half is through the ball. For all the other players not in the scrum, the offside line is an imaginary line drawn through the hindmost foot of the last player in the scrum (*see* fig. 12, page 32). Any player who joins the scrum is offside if he does so from his opponents' side.

The penalty in these cases is a penalty kick awarded to the non-offending team at the place of infringement (subject to the advantage law).

▲ *Fig. 12 Imaginary scrum offside line*

Offside at the ruck and maul

A player is offside at a ruck or maul if he:

- joins it from his opponents' side
- joins it in front of the hindmost player of his team in the ruck or maul
- does not join it but fails to retire behind the offside line without delay
- leaves it and does not immediately retire behind the offside line; or rejoins it in front of the hindmost player of his team in the ruck or maul
- advances beyond the offside line with either foot and does not join the ruck or maul.

The penalty is a penalty kick at the place of infringement.

Offside at the line-out

A player in the line-out is offside if:

- he advances beyond the line of the throw before the ball has touched a player or the ground, unless he does so while jumping for the ball
- after the ball has touched a player or the ground, he advances in front of the ball, unless he is tackling or attempting to tackle an opponent.

If a player is not participating in the line-out he must stand at least 10 m behind the line of touch.

The penalty in the case of the line-out is awarded at least 15 m in from the touch line.

Onside

A player in an offside position in open play can be placed onside (provided he is not within 10 m of or advancing towards an opponent who is waiting to receive the ball or of the place where the ball pitches) by any of the following actions.

- The opponent in possession of the ball has run 5 m. *See* fig. 13, page 34.
- When an opponent has kicked or passed the ball. *See* fig. 14, page 35.
- When an opponent intentionally touches the ball, but does not catch it or gather it.
- An offside player, including one within 10 m of an opponent who is waiting for the ball, is put onside when a player of his own team in possession of the ball has run in front of him (provided the offside player is retiring out of the 10 m area and is not advancing towards the opponents when he is put onside). *See* fig. 15, page 35.
- An offside player becomes onside when a player of his own team who is behind him kicks the ball and then runs in front of him. The kicker and any other onside player can put the player onside. The onside player must be in the field of play or the in-goal, although he can follow up in touch or in touch-in-goal and return to the field of play or in-goal to put the player onside. *See* fig. 16, page 36.
- An offside player becomes onside when he runs behind the player of his own team kicking or carrying the ball.

▼ *Fig.13 Player A kicks the ball forwards, placing his team mate B in an offside position. Player X of the opposition catches the ball, and when he has run 5 m, B (who has not advanced) becomes onside and may tackle him*

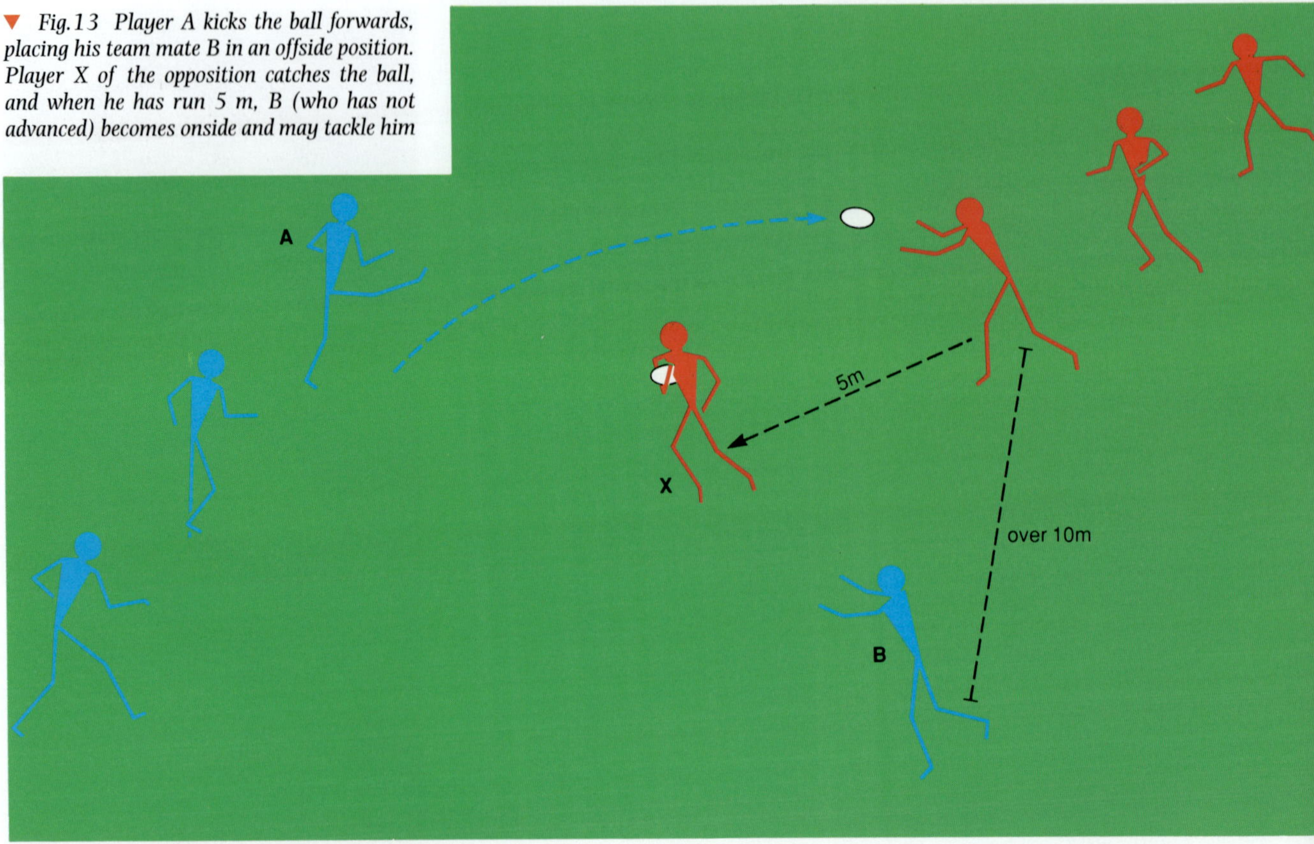

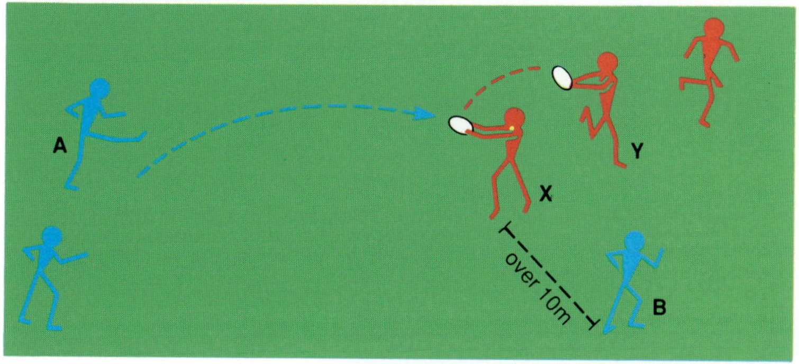

◀ *Fig.14 Player B is offside when his team mate A kicks the ball. The ball is caught by player X of the opposition, who passes it to his team mate Y. Player B, who is not within 10 m of and is not advancing towards X, is put onside by X's pass to Y*

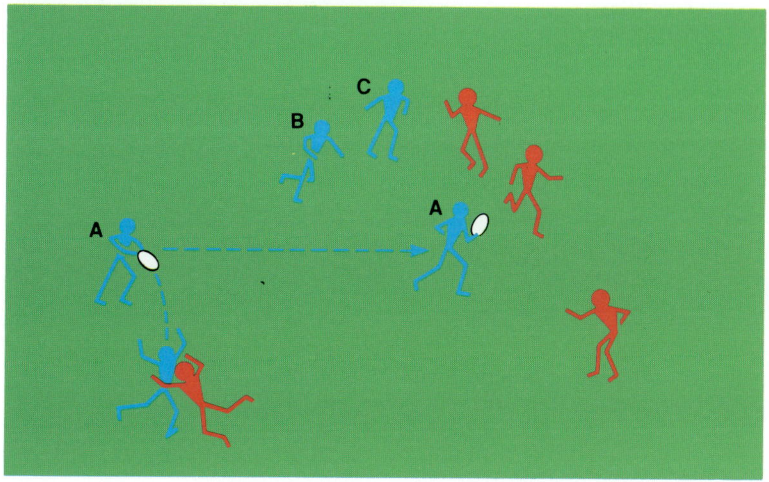

▶ *Fig.15 When player A receives the ball, his team mates B and C are offside. However, as A runs forwards with the ball in his possession he moves ahead of B and C, placing them onside*

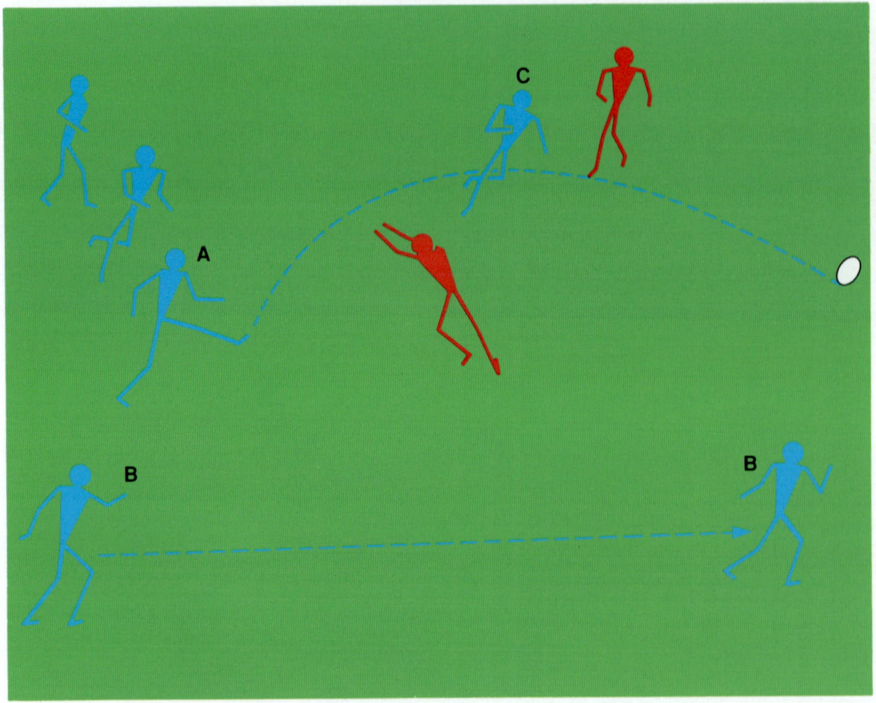

▲ *Fig.16 Player A kicks the ball and runs in front of his team mate C (who is not advancing) to make him onside. Player B of the same team runs forwards and does likewise*

Ball touching referee

If the ball, or a player carrying it, touches the referee in the field of play, a scrum is taken at that spot, unless the referee considers that neither team has gained an advantage, in which case he allows play to proceed.

If the ball, or a player carrying it, touches the referee in the player's in-goal, play continues unless the referee considers that that player's team has gained an advantage, in which case a touch down is awarded at the spot. If the ball or a player carrying the ball in his opponents' in-goal touches the referee, play continues unless the referee considers that that player's team has gained an advantage, in which case a try is awarded at that spot.

The following laws apply if the ball, while in play in in-goal (at either end) and not held by a player, touches the referee or a touch judge:

- a touch down is awarded if it would otherwise have been obtained, or the ball would have gone dead
- a try is awarded if it would otherwise have been obtained.

Obstruction

Obstruction occurs when a player:

- who is running for the ball, charges an opponent (except shoulder to shoulder) also running for the ball
- with the ball in his possession after it has come out from a ruck, scrum or line-out, attempts to force his way through his own forwards
- who is offside, 'shields' a member of his own team, who is carrying the ball, from an opponent
- who is on the outside of the scrum, moves outwards, and even though he maintains contact with the scrum, thereby prevents an opponent getting round the scrum.

For any of these offences, a penalty kick is awarded at the place of infringement.

Misconduct and dangerous play

Foul play is prohibited. Players must not:

- hack, trip or strike an opponent
- tackle early, late or dangerously
- charge or obstruct an opponent who has just kicked the ball
- hold, push, charge, obstruct or grasp an opponent not in possession of the ball, except in a scrum, ruck or maul
- cause a scrum, ruck or maul to collapse
- commit any form of misconduct.

For any of these offences the referee awards a penalty kick at the place of infringement (or in the case of the late charging of a kicker, either at the place of infringement or where the ball lands, at the option of the non-offending team). He will caution the player, and he may order the player off the field. In the event of that player repeating the offence, the referee will order him off the field.

Variations of the game

Seven-a-side

Seven-a-side rugby (or 'sevens') is played on the same sized playing area as the normal game. There are only seven players in each team, and the game lasts for seven minutes each way, with one minute for half-time.

It is very difficult to play sevens 'flat out', and the winning team will be the one which can control the tempo and tire the opposition by superior tactics. It is an exciting game to play and watch, and there is little time for recovery after a successful attack.

Possession is the key, and the ideal team contains intelligent and intuitive players who are able to work hard and keep possession. Players without the ball must support their team mate running with it.

Positional play is also vital, and the team should be spread out in order to provide immediate cover whenever required.

Mini and midi rugby

The Rugby Football Union has devised a series of variations of the 15-a-side game, so that young children can be introduced to the sport through appropriate methods. These variations, a range of games for age groups under-7 to under-12, make up the 'Continuum of Rugby Football'. Its long term aim is to encourage children to progress to the full game by the age of 13.

The game's participants are grouped into age ranges from under-7 to under-12. Girls also play, but the contact in the game may mean that mini rugby is not suitable for mixed teams. No mixed rugby is allowed if one of the participants is over the age of 12 on September 1st of the season involved.

The game is played across a conventional pitch.

The following are recommended pitch sizes.

under-7 & under-8	–30 x 20 m – 2 m in-goal area
under-9 & under-10	–59 x 20 m –5 m in-goal area
under-11	–59 x 38 m –5 m in-goal area
under-12	–59 x 43 m – 5 m in-goal area

Except where the following rules amend or adapt the laws of the game to suit the development of young players, the laws of the game shall apply.

Under-7

- The object of the game is to score a try (worth five points) by placing the ball with downward pressure on or behind the opponents' goal line.
- The game is played between teams of not more than seven players.
- It is recommended that a size 4 ball is used.
- The game is started or restarted with a free pass from the centre of the field. The starter's team must be behind the ball (i.e. nearer their own try line than the starter). The opposing team must be 7 m away, nearer its own goal line. Normal play resumes as the pass is made.
- The ball must be passed sideways or backwards. If the ball is passed forwards or knocked on, it goes to the opposition for a free pass restart. Passing should always be done with two hands. If a player fails to catch the ball and it goes to ground, the ball goes to the opposition for a free pass restart.
- If a player running with the ball is touched with two hands below the waist by an opponent, the player must pass the ball as soon as possible and certainly within three strides. It is helpful for the referee to indicate that a 'tackle' has been made by shouting 'Tackled'.
- If a player – legally touched – fails to pass, the ball goes to the opposing team for a free pass restart.
- The first receiver of a free pass restart should start from not more than 2 m behind the passer.
- When a team loses possession of the ball, it must retire 7 m behind the point of the restart, on a line parallel to the goal line.
- When the ball or player carrying the ball goes out of play, the ball goes to the team not responsible for taking the ball out of play, for a free pass restart at the point where the player or ball went out of play.
- A player must not hand-off or fend-off an opponent in any way. The penalty is a free pass restart to the opposition.
- A player may not kick the ball. If he does, possession goes to the opposing team at the point of the kick for a free pass restart.
- After a try has been scored, the game restarts from the centre with a free pass.
- A game will be made up of two halves, each of up to ten minutes duration.

Note In this version of the game there is a total emphasis on running with the ball, evasion, running in support of the ball carrier, passing, and running to touch the ball carrier. There is no tackling, kicking and handing-off, nor are there scrums or line-outs.

Under-8

This version is identical to the under-7 game except in the following respects.

- After February 1st of the season involved, an uncontested three-man scrummage can be introduced.
- After February 1st, practices leading to contact and tackling can be introduced as preparation for the commencement of tackling at under-9. Tackling is not allowed in games.
- The scrum will be made up of three players from each team. The team not responsible for the stoppage will put the ball into the scrummage and be allowed to win it without contact (opponents cannot push or strike for the ball).
- The laws of the game pertaining to the scrum will apply, with the following exception: the back line of the team not putting the ball into the scrum must remain 7 m behind the scrum until normal play resumes, with the exception of the scrum-half who must remain behind the hindmost foot of his forwards until the ball emerges. Normal play will restart when the ball has emerged from the scrummage.
- Following an infringement for 'feeding' the scrum, striking for the ball or pushing in the scrum, a free pass restart is awarded. The offending team must retire 7 m from the point of the restart towards their own goal line.

Under-9

This version is identical to the under-8 game except in the following respects.

- The game is played between teams of nine players, three of whom will form the scrum, six of whom will form the back line. Players should experience playing in all positions.
- If the ball is passed forwards or knocked on, an uncontested scrum is awarded.
- Any player who is running with the ball can be tackled as laid down in the laws of the game. The law on dangerous play must be applied rigorously, and high tackling must be penalised immediately.
- If the ball is not playable immediately after a tackle, an uncontested scrum is awarded to the team not in possession before the tackle.
- The referee should encourage tackler and tackled player to get away from the ball immediately so that the game can continue. Where a ruck or maul occurs, the offside line for players not in the ruck or maul is at the hindmost foot on their side.
- The scrum will be made up of one row of three players from each team. The team not responsible for the stoppage will put the ball into the scrum and must be allowed to win it without contest. (Opponents cannot push or strike for the ball.) With these exceptions, the laws of the game pertaining to the scrum will apply.
- The back line of the team not putting the ball into the scrum must remain 7 m behind the scrum until normal play resumes, with the exception of the scrum half, who must remain behind the hindmost foot of his forwards until the ball emerges.
- Normal play will restart when the ball has emerged from the scrum.
- When the ball or player carrying the ball goes out of the field of play, the game restarts with a free pass 7 m in from touch on the line of touch. The ball goes to the team not responsible for taking the ball out of play.
- Following an infringement for offside, a high or late tackle, obstruction, handing-off, kicking, scrum 'feeding', or striking for the ball and pushing in the scrum, a free pass retsrt is awarded. The offending team must retire 7 m from the point of restart, towards their own goal line.
- A game will be made up of two halves of not more than 15 minutes.
- There is no kicking or handing-off, nor are there any line-outs.

Under-10

This version is identical to the under-9 game except in the following respects.

- If the ball is passed forwards or knocked on, a *contested* scrum is awarded.
- In the event of a strike against the head, the scrum half who has put the ball into the scrum must not follow the ball until it is out of the scrum.
- If the ball or player carrying the ball goes out of play, a line-out (contested) will take place at the point at which the ball or player crossed the touch line.
- The line-out will be made up of no more than two players from each team plus the player throwing the ball in and an immediate opponent who must stand within 2 m of the touch line, and one player from either side in a position to receive the ball (i.e. the scrum half).
- The line-out will extend 2–7 m from the touch line.
- The team not responsible for taking the ball out of play will throw the ball in.
- The offside line for all players not participating in the line-out will be 7 m back from the line of touch parallel to the goal line. They must remain behind the offside line until the line-out has ended.
- There is no kicking or handing-off.

Under-11 – 'midi rugby'

This version is identical to the under-10 game except in the following respects.

- A team is made up of 12 players: five forwards and seven backs. The locks forming the second row of the scrum must bind together with their inside arms, and their outside arms around the hips of the props in the front row.
- After a try has been scored, a further two points are given for a successful conversion.
- The game will start with a kick-off from the centre of the field. The kicker's team must be behind the ball until it has been kicked, and the receiving team must be at least 7 m back from the ball.
- Players may kick the ball directly to touch only in an area 15 m from their own goal line. A player may not 'fly kick' the ball (an indiscriminate and uncontrolled kick at the ball which is usually on the ground). Dribbling the ball is permitted. All the laws of the game pertaining to kicking in open play will apply.
- After a try has been scored, the team can attempt to convert the try into a goal. The kick at goal will take place from anywhere in front of the posts.
- After a try or goal has been scored, the game will restart with a place kick or a drop kick.
- When an infringement occurs as per the laws of the game, a penalty or free kick will be awarded. The opposition must retire at least 7 m towards their own goal line from the place where the kick is awarded.
- There is no hand-off or fend-off. The penalty is a free pass restart, and the opposition must retire 7 m towards their own goal line from the place where the free pass is awarded.
- A game is made up of two halves of 15 minutes each way.

Under-12 – 'midi rugby'

For the 1997-1998 season under-12 midi-rugby will be identical to the under-11 game, except that a game is made up of two halves of 20 minutes. After September 1998, under-12 rugby will be absorbed into junior rugby, and the 15-a-side game will be played.

New image rugby

New image rugby is a form of touch rugby. It is a fast and exciting non-contact game which emphasises running and handling skills. It can be played by boys and girls together.

The rules can be summarised as follows.

- Any number can play, from 12-a-side down to just 3-a-side. The following combinations of players are suggested:

12-a-side – five forwards, seven backs
11-a-side – five forwards, six backs
10-a-side – three forwards, seven backs
9-a-side – three forwards, six backs
8-a-side – three forwards, five backs
7-a-side – three forwards, four backs
6-a-side – two forwards, four backs
5-a-side – two forwards, three backs
4-a-side – one forward, three backs
3-a-side – one forward, two backs

It is important to remember that this is primarily a running and handling game; therefore, generally there should be more backs than forwards.

- The pitch must be of a suitable size and surface. Its size should be reduced in ratio to the number of players.
- The game is started with a free pass, restart tap kick or a kick-off from the halfway line. The starter's team must be behind the ball. The opponents should be at least 7 m away.
- Apart from the kick-off and the penalty tap kick, no kicking is permitted.
- Players may run with the ball, but must pass it backwards.
- There is no tackling. If a defender touches the ball carrier with one hand on either side of his hips, he must immediately pass the ball. If he does not, a free pass restart or a tap penalty is awarded to the opposition.
- Five points are scored by touching the ball down over the try line.
- A player can only be offside at the kick-off, free pass start, a tap penalty, scrum or line-out.
- If a player passes, knocks or drops the ball forwards and it touches the ground, a scrum is awarded.
- No pushing is allowed in the scrum, and the team putting in the ball wins it unopposed.
- If the ball crosses the touch line, play is restarted by a line-out. The ball must be caught above head height by one of the thrower's team mates, i.e. it is unopposed.
- Players are allocated positions in rotation.
- The duration of play depends on the age and ability of the participants.

Under-13 to under-19 rugby

The following variations in the laws for under-19 rugby have been agreed upon for uniform interpretation throughout the world in schools and under-19 rugby.

Substitution

- Up to seven players may be substituted in matches where all players are below the age of 21.
- When a team names seven replacements, four of the seven must cover the following positions: loose head prop, tight head prop, hooker and second row (lock).
- Any player who is so injured that he should not continue playing may be replaced, but if he is he must not resume playing in the match.
- Players who have been substituted may replace an injured player.

Scrummage

- Eight players from each team shall be required to form a scrummage. While the scrummage is in progress each player shall remain bound in the scrummage until it ends. Each front row of a scrummage shall have three players in it at all times. The head of a player in a front row shall not be next to the head of a player of the same team. In the eight-man scrummage the formation must be 3-4-1 with the single player at the back (normally the no.8) packing between the two locks.
- In the interests of safety, each prop should touch on his opponent's upper arm, then pause prior to engagement in the sequence: crouch, touch, pause, engage. When the place of infringement is within 5 m of the touch line or goal line, the scrummage is formed 5 m away from that touch line or goal line.
- Throughout the duration of a scrummage there must be eight players from each side in the scrummage except when these numbers are reduced by: availability; a player ordered off under Law 26; injury.
- Even allowing for the exceptions above, there must never be less than five players from each team in the scrummage.
- The composition of a scrummage if a side is unable to field or maintain a complete team for any reason shall be: if one team is one short, then both scrummages must be a 3-4 formation; if one team is two short, then both scrummages must be a 3-2-1 formation; if one team is three short, then both scrummages must be a 3-2 formation.

• However, in respect of the three front row and two middle row (lock) positions, should a team . . .
– be unable to provide suitably trained replacements for an injured player(s)
– be unable to field suitably trained players at the commencement of or during a match because of the lack of availability of players
– have one or more of the five designated players sent off under Law 26
. . . the referee must order a non-contestable or simulated scrummage which is a normal scrummage except that:
– there is no contest for the ball
– the team putting in the ball must win it
– neither team is permitted to push.
• There shall not be more than eight players in the scrummage.
• It is illegal to push the opposing scrummage more than 1.5 m from the original line towards either goal line. A player must not hold the ball wilfully in the scrummage once control is established at the base of the scrummage.
• A scrummage must not be intentionally wheeled. The referee should stop play if an unintentional wheel reaches 45 degrees.

Offside at scrummage

• Participating players in a formed scrummage must not leave until the scrummage is ended.
• The no.8 is the only player who is permitted to detach and pick up the emerged ball if he is the last man in a 3-4-1 scrummage (as in international law). On his so doing, the scrummage is ended.

Foul play

It is illegal for a team to adopt the following ploys.
• **Flying wedge**. This is a move which usually takes place close to the opponents' goal line, and is initiated by a player either tapping the ball to himself or receiving a short pass, and then driving towards the goal line with his colleagues binding on to either side of him in a 'V' or wedge formation. Frequently the player is isolated illegally by those of his own team in front of him. The dangers inherent in this formation are not for those initiating the move but for those attempting to stop it.
• **Cavalry charge**. This usually occurs when a penalty kick is awarded to the attacking team close to the opponents' goal line. Players of the attacking team line up behind the kicker, spacing themselves across the field in gaps of 1-2 m. On a signal from the kicker they begin to charge forward. Only when they are close to the kicker does he tap the ball and pass it to one of them. The defending team must remain behind a line 10 m from the mark or their own goal line (if nearer) until the ball has been kicked. The move is potentially dangerous.

Body position

Any player at any stage in a scrummage, ruck or maul who has, or causes an opponent to have, his shoulders lower than his hip joint, must be penalised by the immediate award of a free kick to the non-offending team.

The tackle

(Additional notes to help interpretation of Law 18.)

- No advantage shall be played under this law.
- A player is assumed to have fallen wilfully over or on a tackled player unless the referee is absolutely certain that the fall was accidental.
- In the rare instance of an accidental fall, play must be stopped and a scrummage awarded.

Under-13 to under-15

- The scrum half not putting the ball into the scrum must remain behind the mid-line of the scrum until it is ended. If he goes offside a penalty kick is awarded to the opposition.
- Six substitutions can be made.

Note For all the very latest variations to the laws of junior rugby, please contact the Rugby Football Union at the following address.

The Rugby Football Union

For more details on the game of rugby union and for more information on publications, videos and recent law changes, contact the national office of the USA Rugby Football Union, 3595 East Fountain Blvd., Colorado Springs, CO 80910.

Index

advantage law 30

ball 4

choice of end 7
clothing 6
conversion 26-8

dangerous play 37
dead ball 17
duration of play 6

fair catch 14
falling on the ball 11
flag posts 3
footwear 6
forward pass 9
free kick 14
  quick 14

ground 3
grounding the ball 25

half-time 7
handing off 11

International Rugby Football Board 2

kicking 12-16
  drop 12, 14, 27-8
  free 14
  grubber 12
  penalty 15-16, 27-8
  place 13
  punt 12
  tee 8, 28
kick-off 8
knock-on 9

line-out 19, 32

mark *see* fair catch
maul 23-5, 32
midi rugby 38, 43
mini rugby 38-42
misconduct 37

new image rugby 44

obstruction 37
offences 31-7
officials 29-30
offside 31-6
onside 33-6

penalty kick 15-16
  quick 15
penalty try 26
players' positions 4-5

rebound 9
referee 29, 36
replacements 5
ruck 23-5, 32
Rugby Footbal Union 47

scoring 26-8
  goal 27
  try 26
scrum 20, 31
  formations 20
  put-in 21
seven-a-side 38
start of play 7-8
studs 6

tackling 10
throw in 18
  quick 18
touch 17
  -in-goal 17
  judge 30